# At the Pit

By Debbie Croft

Mim sips at the tap.

*Sip, sip, sip.*

Tim is at the pit.

*Pat, pat, pat.*

Is Tim at the mat?

Mim! Mim!

The pit!

# CHECKING FOR MEANING

1.  Where did Mim sip? *(Literal)*

2.  Where did Mim find Tim? *(Literal)*

3.  What was Tim doing at the pit? *(Inferential)*

# EXTENDING VOCABULARY

| | |
|---|---|
| **tap** | Look at the word *tap*. What does the word mean in this story? How else can you use the word *tap*? |
| **pit** | Look at the word *pit*. What is a smaller word within the word *pit*? Can you think of other words that end in *–it*? |
| **mat** | Look at the word *mat*. What word do you make if you add an *s* to *mat*? How does adding the *s* change the meaning of the word? |

# MOVING BEYOND THE TEXT

1. What activities do people do at a gym?

2. What else do people do to stay fit?

3. What do you do to keep fit?

4. Would you like to try the activities Mim and Tim were doing at the gym? Why or why not?

# SPEED SOUNDS

| Mm | Ss | Aa | Pp | Ii | Tt |

## PRACTICE WORDS

Mim

sips

at

tap

Sip

Tim

sip

pit

pat

Pat

mat

am